Malcolm X

CORNERSTONES OF FREEDOM

SECOND SERIES

Renee Graves

Children's Press®
A Division of Scholastic Inc.
New York • Toronto • London • Auckland • Sydney
Mexico City • New Delhi • Hong Kong
Danbury, Connecticut

Photographs © 2003: AP/Wide World Photos: 5, 9, 12 top, 23, 24, 28, 30, 44 top center; Corbis Images: cover top, 12 bottom, 13, 27, 34, 40 (Bettmann), cover bottom (UPI); Getty Images/Berenice Abbott/Museum of the City of New York: 10; Hulton/Archive/Getty Images: 3, 6, 7, 11, 15, 20, 29, 38, 41, 44 bottom left; Library of Congress: 4; Magnum Photos/Eve Arnold: 26; Scholastic Photo Library: 14, 18 (Richard Saunders), 8, 44 top left (Bruce Perry/Station Hill Press); Stockphoto.com/John Launois: 31, 32, 44 bottom right, 45 bottom left, 45 top right; The Image Works/Topham: 21, 35, 36, 37, 44 top right, 45 top left.

Library of Congress Cataloging-in-Publication Data

Graves, Renee

Malcolm X / Renee Graves.

p. cm. — (Cornerstones of freedom. Second series)

Summary: A biography of Malcolm X, focusing on the incidents that led to his belief that blacks should be willing to use any tactics necessary to secure their freedom and equality.

Includes bibliographical references and index.

ISBN 0-516-24224-5

1. X, Malcolm, 1925–1965—Juvenile literature. 2. Black Muslims—Biography—Juvenile literature. 3. Afro-Americans—Biography—Juvenile literature. [1. X, Malcolm, 1925–1965. 2. Black Muslims—Biography. 3. African Americans—Biography.] I. Title. II. Series: Cornerstones of freedom. Second series.

BP223.Z8L57165 2003

320.54'092—dc21

2003005604

CHILDREN'S PRESS, and CORNERSTONES OF FREEDOM™, and associated logos are trademarks and or registered trademarks of Scholastic Library Publishing. SCHOLASTIC and associated logos are trademarks and or registered trademarks of Scholastic Inc.

1 2 3 4 5 6 7 8 9 10 R 12 11 10 09 08 07 06 05 04 03

I T WAS A COLD FEBRUARY afternoon in New York City, 1965. All eyes in the Audubon Ballroom were focused on the handsome young man standing on the stage. The audience waited as he adjusted the microphone and cleared his throat. There was a hush in the room as he began his speech. Suddenly, shots rang out. The audience screamed as they watched the handsome young man fall to the ground, murdered. Riddled with fifteen bullets, Malcolm X, one of the most influential personalities in American history, was silenced forever.

Malcolm X became the personification of black nationalism. Though intense and controversial, the African-American leader gave his followers hope and pride.

Even after slavery had been abolished in 1865, hate and injustice continued to thrive in America. Black and white communities remained **segregated,** and discrimination against blacks was common practice. Black citizens were forced to use separate drinking fountains, buses, restaurants, theaters, and hospitals. Even cemeteries were separated into black and white sections. In some states, these conditions continued until the 1960s. Having black skin and demanding equality could result in imprisonment or in being lynched by racist white gangs.

MALCOLM'S EARLY YEARS

This was the world that Malcolm Little knew as a child. Malcolm was born in Omaha, Nebraska, in 1925. His father, Earl Little, was an outspoken Baptist preacher who traveled around as a guest speaker in black churches of the area. Little was also an organizer for the Universal Negro Improvement Association, a group founded by a man named Marcus Garvey. The UNIA was founded in order to

Marcus Garvey wears a ceremonial uniform symbolizing black pride during a parade through Harlem for the UNIA around 1920. With millions of members around the world, the UNIA became one of the largest black organizations in history.

THE KLAN

The Ku Klux Klan is a terrorist organization composed of generally poor, rural whites who traditionally wear white robes and hoods that cover their faces. Founded in 1866, they were most active in the 1920s. However, the group regained popularity during the civil rights movement of the 1950s and 1960s. The KKK intimidated black communities by setting crosses ablaze in front of the houses of those black citizens considered to be "troublemakers." They also used threats, beatings, and sometimes resorted to murder in order to terrorize.

An African American, Crispus Attucks, was among the first patriots to die for the cause of American freedom. Yet many black people in the New World were enslaved.

promote Garvey's ideas of black racial purity. Garvey believed that all black people in America should return to their African homeland in order to find equality. Earl Little preached the Baptist faith along with these controversial ideas. Many people in the white community did not like this, and they threatened Little and his family. Windows were broken out of their house and shots were fired at them by the Ku Klux Klan. For safety reasons, Earl Little moved his family to different cities twice before Malcolm was even four years old.

By 1929, the Little family was living in Lansing, Michigan. Earl Little bought a house and was once again preaching and spreading the word of Marcus Garvey. One night while the family was sleeping, arsonists set the house on fire and burned it to the ground. In his autobiography, Malcolm recalled, "I remember being snatched awake into a frightening confusion of pistol shots and shouting and smoke and flames. I remember we were outside in the night in our underwear, crying and yelling our heads off." The men who started the fire were never caught, but it was generally believed that they were members of a local hate society called the Black Legion. This group was very much like the Ku Klux Klan, except that they wore black robes rather than white ones.

Frederick Douglass was an outspoken black leader of the 19th century in America. Malcolm was to find that the contributions of African Americans like Douglass and Attucks were often ignored by educators.

In 1931, when Malcolm was only six years old, his father's **mutilated** body was found lying across a set of streetcar tracks. The death was ruled an accident. Years later, Malcolm stated that he had always believed that the Black Legion had been responsible for both his father's murder as well as the house fire, but there was no way to prove it.

Several years after his father's death, Malcolm received another tragic blow. His mother, Louise, suffered an emotional

Malcolm was an exceptional and popular student during his school days. In his autobiography he recalled one of his fondest memories—being elected class president. "The teacher asked me to leave the room while the class voted. When I returned I was the class president. I couldn't believe it."

breakdown. Louise was a proud woman who hated to receive handouts from neighbors, and her struggle to take care of her eight children alone was more than she could handle. She was declared legally insane and was committed to the State Mental Hospital in Kalamazoo, Michigan, in 1939. Louise remained there for the next twenty-six years.

After his mother was hospitalized, Malcolm and his brothers and sisters were split up and sent off to various foster homes and orphanages. Malcolm was able to continue his schooling in Lansing and was an excellent student. He was the only black child in his junior high class, but he was popular and got along well with both black and white students. However, during his eighth grade year, Malcolm received another blow. Mr. Ostrowski, a white English teacher whom Malcolm particularly admired, asked if Malcolm had considered a career for his future. After learning that Malcolm wanted to be a lawyer, the teacher looked surprised, leaned back in his chair and said, "A lawyer—that's no realistic goal for a nigger. You need to think about something you can be. Why don't you plan on carpentry?" According to Malcolm's account of the incident, that was the moment when he began to change inside.

A LIFE OF CRIME

In 1941, Malcolm dropped out of school and went to live with his half sister, Ella Collins, in Boston, Massachusetts. While in Boston, Malcolm held a variety of menial jobs, including shoe shining, dishwashing, and serving meals in the dining cars of the New Haven Railroad. He also

This is a view of the heart of Boston, Massachusetts, as it looked around the time of Malcolm's first visit in 1940. Having lived in mostly white towns—Omaha, Milwaukee, and Lansing, Michigan—this was Malcolm's first chance to experience a larger black community with a strong identity.

started committing petty crimes in order to supplement this meager income.

By 1942, World War II was underway and Malcolm had moved again—this time to Harlem, New York. Soon, he was drafted by the army. Not really wanting to join the army, Malcolm purposely acted crazy at the induction center, and the psychiatrists rejected him for service. The army declared him "mentally disqualified from military service because of **psychopathic** personality inadequacies."

Malcolm soon became a familiar figure on the streets of Harlem. He became known as "Red" because of the reddish color of his hair. He started wearing brightly colored "zoot suits," smoking marijuana, snorting cocaine, and straightening his hair. He got a job at the Roseland Ballroom, where he was able to see many of the famous jazz artists of the day, including Count Basie, Duke Ellington, and Charlie Barnet. Malcolm also became involved with various narcotic, prostitution, and gambling rings.

Mostly farmland until the mid-19th century, Harlem was at first a destination for European immigrants, followed by members of New York City's elite who were eager to move away from the crowded downtown. Finally, in the early 20th century, it became the country's most famous African-American neighborhood.

Starting in 1934, the Apollo Theater became the best showcase in Harlem for black entertainers, often drawing mixed audiences. This photo, taken around 1941, was how the world-famous New York City landmark looked when Malcolm first came to New York.

Because of his dealings in the criminal underworld of Harlem, Malcolm was forced to move back to Boston in late 1945. He needed to hide from the Mafia, the police, and from another hustler who was planning to kill him. However, Malcolm didn't stay out of trouble in Boston either. He was arrested for robbing a series of houses with his friends and was sentenced to ten years imprisonment. On February 27, 1946, Malcolm began serving his term in prison. He wasn't quite twenty-one years old.

ZOOT SUITS

During the late 1930s and early 40s, certain young people broke the rules of fashion by wearing "zoot suits." Primarily worn by young black and Hispanic men, zoot suits featured long, double-breasted jackets and deeply pleated pants that were extra full, but tapered to a tight cuff. Along with the suit, "zooters" wore shiny two-toned shoes, wide brimmed hats with large feathers dipped over one eye, and long watch fob chains that began at the waist and fell down nearly to the ankles. The zoot suit was a bold fashion statement and wearing it was considered rebellious. Not only did the suits look very unusual next to the mainstream fashion of the day, but they also used up far more fabric than most people thought should be necessary during wartime rationing.

Charlestown State Prison in Massachusetts, where Malcolm was sentenced to ten years in 1946. He was not quite 21 years old at the time. He later said of his prison years that he was glad he was arrested early.

Malcolm was under arrest on a robbery charge at the time this mug shot was taken in Boston, Massachusetts, in 1944.

MALCOLM DISCOVERS ISLAM

Malcolm did not handle prison life well. He found himself without the drugs that he was used to having, and he missed the fast life that he had lived in Harlem. He later said that he would spend his time pacing in his cell "like a caged leopard, viciously cursing aloud to myself. And my favorite targets were the Bible and God." Malcolm was an **atheist** when he entered prison. He later wrote, "I considered myself beyond atheism—I was Satan." In fact, "Satan" was the nickname Malcolm was given by his fellow prisoners because of his angry, anti-religious attitude.

The first person in prison to make a positive impression on Malcolm was another inmate, a black man named "Bimbi." Malcolm noticed that Bimbi commanded total respect from his fellow prisoners—not with his fists, but with his words. Bimbi was able to voice his opinion and speak logically about any subject that came up. He suggested that Malcolm should take advantage of the prison library and take some courses by mail instead of wasting his time cursing the guards and pacing in his cell. Malcolm

When a black soldier was shot by a white policeman on August 1, 1943, at a Harlem hotel, it escalated into one of the worst race riots in New York City's history.

"A race of people is like an individual man; unless it uses its own talent, takes pride in its own history, expresses its own culture . . . it can never fulfill itself," Malcolm taught. Here, Malcolm leads Black Muslim children on a tour of the Museum of Natural History in New York City.

took his advice and began visiting the library, reading as many books as he could find. It was during this time that Malcolm became aware of the one major force that was going to direct the rest of his life—the religious teachings of the Nation of Islam.

Malcolm first heard about the Nation of Islam through letters from his brothers Philbert and Reginald and his sister Hilda. Many members of his family had converted from the Baptist faith to the teachings of a man named Elijah Muhammad. Muhammad was the head of a religious group called The Nation of Islam (or NOI, for short). The NOI considers itself a branch of the religion known as Islam. The people who practice the Islamic faith are called Muslims. Malcolm's brothers claimed that the Nation of Islam was "the natural religion for the black man."

Skeptical at first, Malcolm began reading about the Islamic faith, the Nation of Islam, and Elijah Muhammad in the prison library.

The Nation of Islam began in 1930, when a man named Wallace D. Fard, an African immigrant, began preaching black **nationalism** along with the principles of the Islamic faith in Detroit, Michigan. Fard gathered followers among the poverty-stricken African Americans in his neighborhood. Fard preached that he was "God in person," and a re-creation of Allah (the Islamic term for

14

Malcolm held Elijah Muhammad in the utmost respect. Alex Haley, who helped Malcolm write his autobiography, later commented: "I don't think Malcolm uttered five sentences those early years . . . without saying, 'I have been taught by' or 'All that I know' comes from the Honorable Elijah Muhammad."

15

"God"). One of Fard's followers was a quiet man named Elijah Muhammad. Fard mysteriously disappeared four years after he founded the Nation of Islam, and Elijah Muhammad took over the congregation.

Prisons were the most fertile recruiting ground for the NOI in its early days. Even the harshest critics of the NOI admitted that it was very successful in **rehabilitating** hardened criminals, especially drug addicts, by giving them a sense of discipline and pride.

THE MANY FACES OF ISLAM

The religion of Islam, (from which the Nation of Islam drew its teachings), was founded in the seventh century by a man named Mohammed. Mohammed claimed to have received divine revelations that were gathered together into a book known as the Qur'an, the holy book of Islam. By the time of his death in A.D. 632, Muhammad had spread the teachings of Islam over most of the Middle East.

Although there are now almost 150 branches (or sects) of the Islamic faith, they all have several things in common. Their places of worship are known as mosques, their God is called "Allah," and their holiest leaders are referred to as "**prophets**." All Muslims refrain from eating pork and believe in separating the sexes into two different areas during prayer.

The sects do have important differences, though. In the **orthodox** Islamic faith, the idea that Allah can appear in a physical form on Earth is utterly rejected, while followers of the Nation of Islam believe that Allah appeared in the form of Wallace Fard. Orthodox Islam preaches that there have been many prophets on Earth (including Jesus), but that the Prophet Mohammed was the last and final prophet. However, NOI proclaims that Elijah Muhammad was also a prophet of Allah. Orthodox Islam believes in a life after death, while the NOI does not. Finally, the NOI only accepts members who are of the black race, while Orthodox Islam is universal and welcomes members from all racial and ethnic backgrounds.

The Nation of Islam also differs from Orthodox Islam when it comes to their ideas about the history of the human race. According to Elijah Muhammad and the Nation of Islam, it was written that the white race would rule the world for six thousand years. The black race would then produce a God on earth that would finally show them the evil ways of the whites and lead the black race to a position of power. Elijah Muhammad claimed that the God who appeared on Earth was Wallace D. Fard. Orthodox Islam does not teach these beliefs.

Malcolm was fascinated by the teachings of Elijah Muhammad. While in prison, he wrote a letter to Muhammad and was very pleased to receive a reply welcoming him into the faith. By the time Malcolm was paroled in 1952, he was a new man. He changed his name to Malcolm X, because he now considered Little to be a "slave name." He used the X as a substitute to signify his lost African tribal name. Malcolm X had completely changed himself from a drug-dealing burglar into a devout member of the Nation of Islam.

AN INSPIRATIONAL LIFE

There was a tremendous revival of interest in the life of Malcolm X when director Spike Lee released his movie *Malcolm X* in 1992. The screenplay for the movie was based on the *Autobiography of Malcolm X*. Denzel Washington was nominated for a best actor Oscar for his portrayal of Malcolm.

A DEVOUT LIFE

After leaving prison, Malcolm went to Detroit and lived with his brother Wilfred. He began attending NOI meetings three times a week and was frequently asked to travel to Chicago to stay with Elijah Muhammad while taking lessons to become a NOI minister. Malcolm recruited new people into the faith and tripled the NOI membership after only a

Malcolm is most remembered as an outspoken leader, yet as a minister he had many other important duties. Here, he meets with a young couple to counsel them about a personal problem.

few months. Malcolm was soon named the new assistant minister of Detroit Temple Number One. (It was not until 1961 that NOI members began using the term "mosques.") Elijah Muhammad realized that the eloquent, eager, and enthusiastic young minister was an important asset to the Nation of Islam.

Malcolm was soon traveling to many different cities, including Boston, Philadelphia, and New York, in order to recruit new members to the faith and set up new temples. During this time, Malcolm's idolization of his "Master," Elijah Muhammad, continued to grow. In a magazine article, Malcolm said "no man on earth today is his equal. Whatever I am that is good, it is through what I have been taught by Mr. Muhammad."

Malcolm quickly became the NOI's most effective minister. He became well known for forceful sermons that described the exploitation of black people by the white race. He scoffed at the civil rights movement and rejected the ideas of **integration** and racial equality. Instead, he called for black pride, separation, and self-reliance among members of the black community. Because he supported the use of violence (for self-defense), Malcolm was labeled as a **fanatic** by most of mainstream America, and his leadership was dismissed by many civil rights leaders of the day. Martin Luther King, Jr., one of the most well-respected defenders of civil rights in America, said of Malcolm X, "I know that I have often wished that he would talk less of violence, because violence is not going to solve our problem."

Congressman Adam Clayton Powell, Jr., (right), from Harlem, New York, was one of the first elected leaders to make civil rights an issue. Here, he stands with A. Philip Randolph, the head of the Brotherhood of Sleeping Car Porters, a labor union that became an early symbol of the African-American struggle for dignity, respect, and a decent livelihood.

★ ★ ★ ★

In 1956, a young woman named Betty Jean Sanders joined the New York branch of the NOI. Betty was originally from Detroit and worked as a nurse. After joining the NOI, she changed her name to Betty X, and soon attracted the attention of Malcolm X. In late 1957, Malcolm told Elijah Muhammad that he planned to marry Betty X. In January of 1958, while he was travelling for the NOI, Malcolm telephoned Betty from a gas station phone booth in Detroit and proposed to her. Betty accepted. A justice of the peace married the couple two days later in Lansing, Michigan. They drove back to New York and moved into a three-room apartment in Queens. Attallah, their first daughter, was born the following November.

MALCOLM GAINS NATIONAL ATTENTION

Unlike Elijah Muhammad, Malcolm didn't shy away from publicity. He began giving speeches all over the United States and his name seemed to be constantly in the newspapers. His speeches were also often broadcast on the radio. Soon he was drawing audiences that numbered over ten thousand people.

The time was right for a speaker like Malcolm to come to the nation's attention. In 1955, Rosa Parks, a black seamstress, refused to give up her seat in the "white section" of a bus in Montgomery, Alabama. She was arrested, and in response, civil rights leaders organized the Montgomery bus boycott of 1955–1956. This was the first major event of the civil rights movement in America.

NONVIOLENCE VS. VIOLENCE

The civil rights movement was not a series of boycotts and sit-ins. Even though leaders like Martin Luther King, Jr., preached nonviolence, there were violent outbursts. Many whites were not committed to nonviolence. Police forces in both Mississippi and Alabama murdered civil rights workers, and local governments turned high-pressure fire hoses and set attack dogs on protesters.

Malcolm speaks at a Harlem rally in June 1963. Shortly before his assassination, Malcolm told his biographer Alex Haley, "the [white man] will make use of me dead, as he has made use of me alive, as a convenient symbol of 'hatred'—and that will help him to escape facing the truth that all I have been doing is holding up a mirror to reflect . . . the history of unspeakable crimes that his race has committed against my race."

By 1959, the movement threatened to divide the country. White politicians who believed in segregation were in control of most of southern America, and the South became a civil rights battleground. The state of race relations in America was at an all-time low.

It was in this tense atmosphere that Malcolm began to get noticed—both by black audiences, who usually responded well to him, and by white audiences, who usually feared him. Malcolm urged black people to arm themselves in self-defense against the white establishment. In one speech, Malcolm told his audience, "our religion teaches us to be intelligent. Be peaceful, be courteous, obey the law, respect everyone; but if someone lays a hand on you, send him to the cemetery." As racial tension in America grew, so did the crowds that followed Malcolm.

Large crowds in auditoriums were not the only people listening to the words of Malcolm X, however. The FBI considered Malcolm (along with other outspoken black activists) to be a possible threat to the safety of the United States. Because the government felt the need to monitor his activities and his words, secret agents were assigned to join the NOI disguised as new members. One of these secret agents even worked as Malcolm's bodyguard. Listening devices (bugs) and secret cameras were placed in Malcolm's offices and in the meeting rooms of the NOI. He was also followed at all times. The file that the FBI kept on Malcolm continued to grow until his death.

Malcolm X entered white America's awareness through his close association with the outspoken new world heavyweight boxing champion, Cassius Clay. Malcolm was held responsible for converting Clay to the Nation of Islam, which led Clay to change his name to Muhammad Ali.

THINGS FALL APART

Since Malcolm had always idolized Elijah Muhammad, what happened next was especially hard on him. According to Malcolm, Elijah Muhammad and other high officials of the NOI grew increasingly jealous of him. Negative comments were made about Malcolm's growing power, and rumors spread that he was trying to take over the leadership of the NOI. Malcolm also learned that an order had been issued stating that news about him was not to be published in the official NOI newspaper. These problems continued on

and off for several years. They hurt Malcolm very much, but he tried to ignore them and carry on with his work.

However, Malcolm's faith in Elijah Muhammad was shaken once again when he heard rumors that Muhammad had committed **adultery** with several of his personal secretaries, and that the women claimed that Muhammad was the father of four of their children. Malcolm considered Muhammad to be black America's supreme moral leader, but actions such as these were strictly forbidden by the Islamic faith. Malcolm found it impossible to think that Muhammad could commit such a sin, and he refused to believe the rumors for months. However, many of the members of the mosque in Chicago were leaving the faith after hearing about Muhammad's behavior. When Malcolm finally discovered that the rumors were indeed true, he was completely disillusioned.

Malcolm did his best to avoid making negative statements about Muhammad in the press, however, fearing that it would be harmful to the Nation of Islam. He continued to throw himself into his work, and made headlines after he criticized the way President John F. Kennedy dealt with racial riots in Birmingham, Alabama. He also attended the civil rights march in Washington, D.C., in August 1963. He decided to go to the demonstration as an observer, not as a speaker, however. He was upset because Martin Luther King, Jr., and other **pacifist** black leaders had taken over the organization of the march, and according to Malcolm, ". . . as they took it over, it lost its militancy. It ceased to be angry . . ."

In November 1963, President Kennedy was assassinated in Dallas, Texas. The nation was shocked and deeply saddened. Elijah Muhammad immediately issued an order that no comments at all were to be made by any NOI ministers concerning the assassination. Malcolm was speaking in

THE MARCH ON WASHINGTON

On August 28, 1963, many Americans witnessed over 250,000 black and white people united for the first time—marching, singing, and celebrating side by side, all for the cause of civil rights. The coordinators of the March on Washington agreed that the goals of the march would include the passage of the Civil Rights Act, the integration of public schools, the passage of a law ending job discrimination, and a demand for job training. At the time, it was the largest demonstration for human rights in the history of America. Many fiery speeches were made, but the most famous was made by Martin Luther King, Jr., the often-quoted "I Have a Dream" speech. The march was a great success, drawing major media attention with no violence. To people tired of racial discrimination, bombings, murders, and fear, the March on Washington gave them a reason to hope.

New York City several days later, and when asked what he thought about Kennedy's assassination, he told the group exactly what he thought, despite Muhammad's order to be silent. Malcolm said that he believed that ". . . the hate in white men had not stopped with the killing of defenseless black people, but that hate, allowed to spread unchecked, finally had struck down this country's chief of staff." Malcolm also added that he saw the assassination as a case of ". . . the chickens coming home to roost." This statement made headlines all over the world.

The next day Malcolm met with a very angry Elijah Muhammad. Malcolm was "silenced" by the NOI for ninety days. He was forbidden to talk to the press or to teach in his mosque. Malcolm did not like being censored, but he

Malcolm's immense popularity and his disagreements with Elijah Muhammad would eventually divide the Nation of Islam.

26

accepted the order without a fight. Rumors started to spread that some people in the NOI wanted him dead. Malcolm believed that Elijah Muhammad was probably the one responsible for starting the rumors, and he was completely devastated to think that the man whom he had idolized for so many years now wanted him dead. Malcolm said, "The death talk was not my fear. The thing worse than death was the betrayal."

A NEW ORGANIZATION

By 1964, Malcolm was seriously questioning his future with the Nation of Islam. However, he was still very busy during this period. In January 1964, he agreed to be interviewed for a few months by author Alex Haley, so that Haley could help Malcolm write his autobiography. Malcolm also spoke

TWO GIANTS MEET

Although Malcolm X and Martin Luther King, Jr., were two of the most famous black leaders in America in the 1960s, they only met each other in person once. The meeting took place by accident, when they both happened to be in attendance as the Civil Rights Act was debated in Congress on March 26, 1964.

The two most powerful voices of the civil rights era, Martin Luther King, Jr., and Malcolm X in 1964. Each man respected the other, although they disagreed on the means by which freedom and justice should be achieved for African Americans.

at Harvard University and conducted numerous radio and television interviews. During this time, Malcolm began distancing himself from the NOI. He even began to cautiously speak out against Elijah Muhammad and his "immorality." In response, Elijah Muhammad demanded the return of Malcolm's home and car, both of which had been given to Malcolm and his family by the NOI. Malcolm also began to receive a large number of anonymous death threats.

Malcolm began thinking about starting a new group of his own. Each day more and more disgruntled followers of Elijah Muhammad announced their break with the NOI and

Malcolm X was an admirer of another revolutionary of the time—Che Guevara. Trained as a doctor, Che fought to liberate the oppressed lower classes in Latin America. Besides helping Fidel Castro overthrow Cuba's dictatorship in the 1950s, Che fought for revolution in such places as the Congo and Bolivia.

eagerly pledged their support to Malcolm instead. Encouraged by this, Malcolm formally resigned from the Nation of Islam on March 8, 1964, and announced the formation of his new group, the "Muslim Mosque, Inc." Unlike the Nation of Islam, this organization was committed to gaining political power in order to achieve their goals. In addition, this group pledged to support and cooperate with other established civil rights leaders.

Shortly after Malcolm formed the Muslim Mosque, Inc., he founded another political organization, the Organization of Afro-American Unity (OAAU). The main purpose of this

29

On February 4, 1965, in Selma, Alabama, Malcolm spoke at Browns Chapel to young black people involved in the voter registration protests. Dr. Martin Luther King, along with 250 other protesters, was in jail at the time. Malcolm spoke to the crowd about the magnitude of the struggle for civil rights—not just in the South or the North, but around the globe.

group was to bring the plight of the African-American citizen to the attention of the United Nations. Malcolm hoped that by bringing the civil rights campaign to the attention of international organizations, other countries might pressure the Unites States into making more progress. In one of Malcolm's most famous speeches, he explained, "We want freedom by any means necessary. We want justice by any means necessary. We want equality by any means necessary . . . The thing that I would like to impress upon every Afro-American leader is that no kind of action in this country is ever going to bear fruit unless that action is tied in with the overall international struggle."

"You may be shocked by these words coming from me but [this pilgrimage] has forced me to re-arrange much of my thought patterns previously held, and toss aside some of my previous conclusions." So Malcolm wrote after making his pilgrimage to Mecca.

THE HAJJ

Mecca is the birthplace of Mohammed the Prophet, and Muslims consider it to be the holiest city in the world. It is located in northwest Saudi Arabia and sits in a narrow valley overlooked by hills crowned with castles. Each year, thousands of Muslim pilgrims come from all over the world to worship Allah in Mecca. This is known as "The Hajj" and every devout Muslim is supposed to attempt this journey at least once during their lifetime. Financial assistance is even provided to poor Muslims to insure they partake in this holiest of pilgrimages.

A PILGRIMAGE TO MECCA

In the spring of 1964, Malcolm flew to Boston to visit his sister Ella. Malcolm told her that he had decided to go on a religious **pilgrimage** to Mecca, and Ella agreed to finance

Before going to Mecca, Malcolm spent time sightseeing in Cairo, Egypt. Upon meeting Muslims bound on the pilgrimage, Malcolm said, "They were of all complexions, the whole atmosphere was of warmth and friendliness. The feeling hit me that there wasn't really a color problem here . . . I thought I had just stepped out of prison."

his trip. In April of that year, Malcolm left for the Middle East. During this pilgrimage, Malcolm had his next life-changing experience. In Mecca, Malcolm saw thousands of pilgrims from all over the world—people of all colors, from blue-eyed blondes to black-skinned Africans. He was truly astounded by the "sincere and true brotherhood practiced by all colors together, irrespective of their color."

＊　＊　＊　＊

Malcolm wrote letters home from Mecca explaining that his trip had forced him to change his mind about many of the things that he had believed in the past, including his attitude toward whites. When asked later how these ideas had been changed by his pilgrimage, Malcolm said, "in the past, yes, I have made sweeping indictments of all white people. I will never be guilty of that again—as I know now that some white people are truly sincere, that some truly are capable of being brotherly toward a black man. The true Islam has shown me that a blanket **indictment** of all white people is as wrong as when whites make blanket indictments against blacks."

After returning to the United States, Malcolm's new "spiritual awakening" was big news. His black militant views, which blamed whites for all of the problems that blacks incurred in society, seemed to have reversed. Instead, he now embraced a more Orthodox Islamic view that stressed tolerance. Malcolm also formally stopped using the Nation of Islam symbol of "X" in his name. He let everyone know that he was now to be called by a more traditional Orthodox Islamic name, "Malik El-Shabazz," and that his wife should now be referred to as "Betty Shabazz." However, his troubles with Elijah Muhammad and the NOI were not yet over.

THE NATION OF ISLAM TODAY

After Elijah Muhammad's death in 1975, the Nation of Islam was led by Muhammad's son, Wallace D. Muhammad. Wallace moved the NOI toward a more traditional, orthodox type of Islamic belief. The group changed its name to the American Muslim Society and began to accept members of all races. However, in 1977, Louis Farrakhan, a former follower of Elijah Muhammad, split away from this group and reformed the Nation of Islam, re-establishing many of the NOI's controversial views about race and society. Farrakhan continues to lead the NOI today.

33

Early in the morning of Sunday, February 14, 1965, Malcolm's home was firebombed. Luckily, Malcolm and his family escaped unharmed. He blamed the bombings on the Muslims associated with Elijah Muhammad.

A VOICE IS SILENCED

In 1964, Elijah Muhammad sued to have Malcolm and his family evicted from their house on Long Island, New York. On the next day, *The New York Herald Tribune* reported that

Malcolm and his family had been put under police protection because of the numerous death threats that they had received. During the next several months, there were various attacks made against Malcolm's life. In spite of these assassination attempts, Malcolm traveled to Africa, made a trip to Oxford, England, and spoke at the Harvard Law School Forum. On Valentine's Day, 1965, Malcolm's house was firebombed, but he and his family escaped unharmed.

Seven days following the firebombing, Malcolm arrived at the Audubon Ballroom in Harlem to give a speech to the OAAU. His pregnant wife and four daughters sat at a table

Betty Shabazz, Malcolm's widow, leaves the morgue with her lawyer after identifying her husband's body. "What should be remembered about Malcolm is his love of humanity, his willingness to work." Betty said years later. " He did all of the things that he had to do and should have done."

Malcolm is rushed from the Audubon Ballroom at 166th Street to the Columbia-Presbyterian Hospital in New York City on February 21, 1965, after being gunned down on stage. The leader was pronounced dead shortly thereafter.

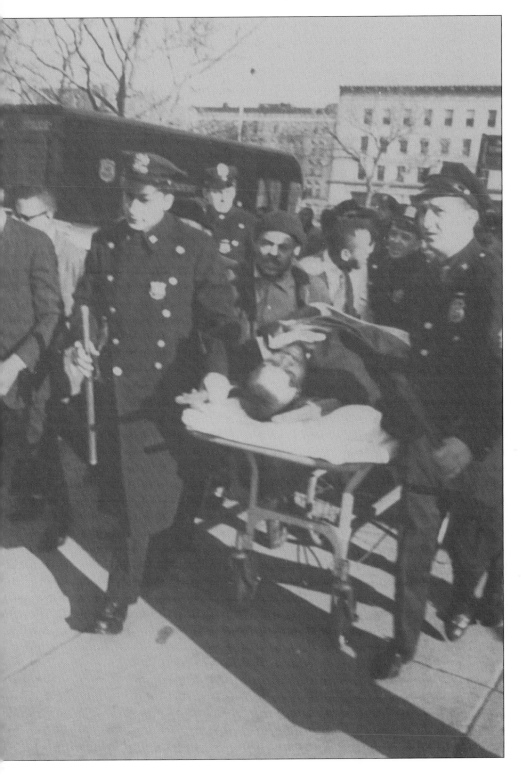

★ ★ ★ ★

On the experience of hearing Malcolm speak, Sonia Sanchez, a poet and civil rights activist, said, "He knew how to, in a very real sense, open your eyes to the kind of oppression that you were experiencing."

near the stage. As Malcolm began to speak, three black gunmen rushed toward him and shot him fifteen times at close range. Betty Shabazz pushed her daughters down under the table and covered them with her own body. The 39-year-old black leader was pronounced dead on arrival at New York's Columbia Presbyterian Hospital. More than fifteen hundred people attended his funeral six days later in Harlem. Ossie Davis, a famous playwright and actor, presided over the service. After the ceremony, Malcolm's black friends took the shovels from the hands of the white gravediggers and buried his casket themselves. Several months later, Betty Shabazz gave birth to twin daughters.

In March 1966, three men were convicted for murdering Malcolm: Talmadge Hayer, Norman 3X Butler, and Thomas 15X Johnson. All three were members of the Nation of Islam. In an interview conducted the day after Malcolm's murder, Elijah Muhammad said that neither he nor the NOI had anything to do with the death, and expressed his "shock and surprise" at the murder.

Martin Luther King, Jr., sent a telegram to Betty Shabazz expressing his condolences. In the telegram, he told her that he was sorry to hear about "the shocking and tragic assassination of your husband. He was an eloquent spokesman for his point of view and no one can honestly doubt that Malcolm had a great concern for the problems we face as a race."

Although Malcolm had been murdered before he could fully develop his new spiritual conversion, his message was still clear: "I am not a racist in any form whatever. I don't believe in any form of racism. I don't believe in any form of discrimination or segregation. I believe in Islam." Though controversial and often fear-provoking, Malcolm had voiced the honest anger that a race of people had been forced to keep to themselves for hundreds of years. He lives on as a symbol of pride, integrity, and confidence and still influences people in every walk of life.

Ossie Davis—playwright, actor, director—gives the eulogy at Malcolm's funeral on February 27, 1965, in New York City. "Malcolm was . . . our own black shining Prince who did not hesitate to die because he loved us so."

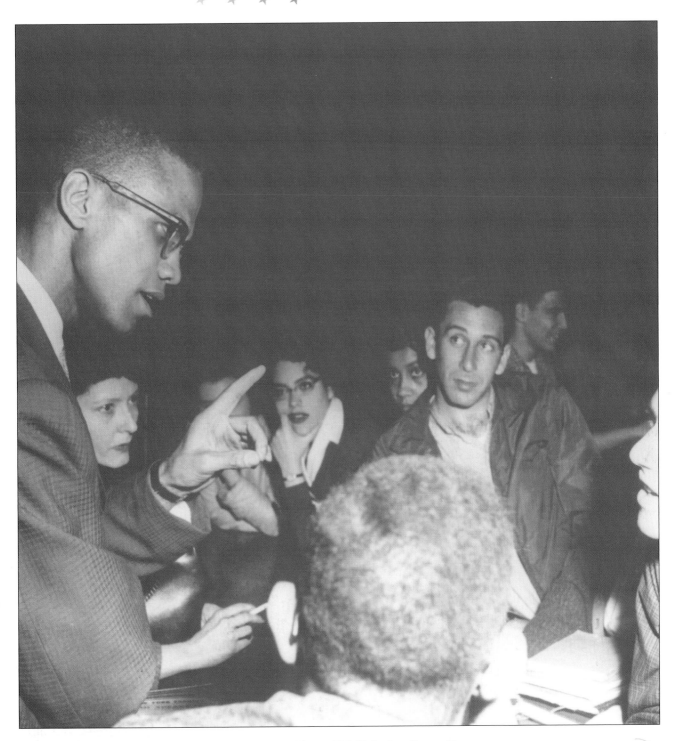

"Without education, you are not going anywhere in this world," Malcolm often said.
Here, he lectures at Queens College in New York.

41

Glossary

adultery—to have sexual relations with a person who is not your husband or wife

atheist—a person who does not believe in the existence of God

fanatic—a person whose beliefs make him or her seem dangerous to others

indictment—an expression of strong disapproval

integration—the mixture of different races or types of people in society as equals

mutilate—to cut up, cut off, or maim

nationalism—extreme pride in one's country, race, or ethnic background

orthodox—the most conventional or common form of a religion's teachings, practices, or beliefs

pacifist—a believer in non-violence

pilgrimage—a trip made by a religious believer to a
place considered holy or special in that religion

prophet—in religious belief, someone who speaks God's
words to other humans

psychopathic—in psychology, a disturbed state of being
characterized by extreme disregard for others and
the constant pursuit of personal desires, often
through criminal behavior

rehabilitating—the process of bringing an individual
back to health or productive activity

segregation—the separation of different races, groups,
or types of people in society

Timeline: Malcolm X

1925

Malcolm Little is born in Omaha, Nebraska, on May 19.

1934

Elijah Muhammad becomes the leader of the Nation of Islam.

1941

Malcolm moves to Boston to live with his half-sister Ella.

1946

Malcolm begins serving a prison term.

1952

Malcolm is paroled from prison as a convert to the Nation of Islam.

1955

Rosa Parks refuses to leave her seat on a Montgomery, Alabama, bus, sparking the national civil rights movement.

1958

Malcolm marries Betty Sanders.

Malcolm begins to question Elijah Muhammad's authority as leader of the Nation of Islam.

Malcolm begins work on his autobiography and splits with the Nation of Islam.

Malcolm becomes the most well-known spokesman for the Nation of Islam.

Malcolm is assassinated in the Audubon Ballroom in Harlem on February 21.

Spike Lee's film *Malcolm X* creates new interest in Malcolm's life, especially among the young.

To Find Out More

BOOKS

Brown, Kevin. *Malcolm X: His Life and Legacy.* Brookfield, CT: Millbrook Press, 1995.

Crushshon, Theresa. *Malcolm X: Journey to Freedom.* Chanhassen, MN: Child's World, 2001.

Diamond, Arthur. *Malcolm X: A Voice for Black America.* Berkeley Heights, NJ: Enslow, 1994.

Draper, Allison Stark. *The Assassination of Malcolm X.* New York, NY: Rosen Publishing Group, Inc., 2002.

Malcolm X. *Malcolm X Talks to Young People.* New York, NY: Pathfinder Press, 2001.

Myers, Walter Dean. *Malcolm X: By Any Means Necessary: A Biography.* New York, NY: Scholastic, 1994.

ONLINE SITES

The Museum of Malcolm X Website
http://www.themalcolmxmuseum.org/

The Official Website of Malcolm X
http://www.cmgww.com/historic/malcolm/

Twenty-First Century Books
http://www.brothermalcolm.net/

Index

A llah, 16

Audubon Ballroom, 3, 35–37

B imbi, 13

Black Legion, 6–7

Black Muslims see Nation of Islam

C ivil rights movement, 21–22, 25

Collins, Ella, 8

D avis, Ossie, 37

E lijah Muhammad, 14–20, 23–28, 33–35, 37

F ard, Wallace D., 14–17

G arvey, Marcus, 5–6

H aley, Alex, 27

Hajj, 31–32

I slam, 14, 16, 31–33, 40

K ennedy, John F., 25–26

King, Martin Luther, Jr., 19, 21, 25, 28, 39

Ku Klux Klan, 6

L ittle, Earl, 4–7

Little, Ella, 31–32

Little, Hilda, 14

Little, Louise, 7–8

Little, Philbert, 14

Little, Reginald, 14

Little, Wilfred, 18

M alcolm X,

breaks with Nation of Islam, 23–27

changes name, 18, 33

childhood, 4–8

conversion to Islam, 14–20

death, 3

life of crime, 8–11

makes hajj, 31–32

marries, 20

prison, 12–18

surveillance, 22

March on Washington, 25

Mecca, Saudi Arabia, 31–33

Mohammed, 16

N ation of Islam, 14–20, 26–29, 33, 39–40

O rganization of Afro-American Unity, 29

P arks, Rosa, 21

Q ur'an, 16

S anders, Betty Jean see Shabazz, Betty

Segregation, 4, 22

Shabazz, Betty, 20, 33, 39

U niversal Negro Improvement Association, 5

About the Author

Renee Graves is a freelance writer who lives in Memphis, Tennessee. She has a background in journalism and has worked for newspapers in Texas and Mississippi. She has also worked as a middle and high school English teacher and most recently taught creative writing part-time at a local university. She is the author of several books on American history for young readers.